Sterling Publishing Co., Inc.
New York

# Celebrating
# PEZ®

By Nina Chertoff and Susan Kahn

Published by Sterling Publishing Co., Inc.
387 Park Avenue South, New York, NY 10016

© 2006 Nina Chertoff and Susan Kahn

Distributed in Canada by Sterling Publishing
c/o Canadian Manda Group, 165 Dufferin Street,
Toronto, Ontario, Canada M6K 3H6

Distributed in the United Kingdom by GMC Distribution Services,
Castle Place, 166 High Street, Lewes, East Sussex, England BN7 1XU

Distributed in Australia by Capricorn Link (Australia) Pty. Ltd.
P.O. Box 704, Windsor, NSW 2756, Australia

ISBN-13: 978-1-4027-4227-9
ISBN-10: 1-4027-4227-4

Printed in China

10  9  8  7  6  5  4  3  2  1

For information about custom editions, special sales, premium and
corporate purchases, please contact Sterling Special Sales
Department at 800-805-5489 or specialsales@sterlingpub.com.

This book is in no way affiliated with PEZ® Candy, Inc.
PEZ® is a registered trademark of Patrafico AG, Inc.

# Contents

# Introduction

"Want one?" That's the anthem of the PEZ world. It is impossible to hold that little giraffe or Winnie-the-Pooh or cowboy dispenser in your hand without tipping back the head and pushing the candy forward.

Welcome to the world of PEZ. And what a world it is: aglow with color and inhabited by animals, ghosts, witches, superheroes, circus characters, brides and grooms, Mickey Mouse, Tweety Bird, and hundreds of other beguiling characters. There's something about these little plastic figures that reaches out and pulls you in whether you are five or ninety-five.

PEZ is everywhere these days and has been for many decades. If you are a baby boomer, you might remember the early ones from the 1950s that had flat tops instead of heads. Too bad you threw them out; those old plain PEZ dispensers are now worth hundreds, sometimes even thousands of dollars. Your kids probably collected them too, Halloween pumpkins or Star Wars characters and the Simpsons clan. For many kids, PEZ dispensers are the first thing they collect, and it's easy to start since dispensers are so inexpensive— sometimes just a dollar or two.

One very rare and valuable PEZ, shown above, was made for a Lions Club meeting in Nice, France, in 1962. The Lion was specially inscribed for the meeting. Today, this dispenser can fetch $2,500 or more. On the right are Donald Duck, Eeyore, and Tweety Bird.

**A**bove is one of the Merry Music Makers produced in the early 1980s. A whistle is attached to the back of the Rhino's head. Donald Duck with a die-cut stem is at near right, and on far right is Obelix, a popular European comic book character.

While PEZ seem ubiquitous to Americans, they actually were first developed in Vienna, Austria, in 1927 by Edward Haas. Haas was a man who disliked everything about smoking. He decided to manufacture a mint that might replace smoking for some people, while serving committed smokers as a breath mint—a brand-new concept. Haas used a new peppermint oil from England to flavor his mint, and PEZ was born. The word PEZ, in fact, comes from the German word for mint: *pfefferminz*. The first, middle, and last letters spell out PEZ. Since Haas wanted a mint that could easily be mass-produced, he made it rectangular, an economical shape to manufacture.

The mints were first sold in a little tin, and if you can find one of those today, you'll see that they are quite valuable. Eventually Haas decided that his mints should be placed in a hygienic container. In 1948, he developed just such a dispenser. It looked like a cigarette lighter, which seemed appropriate, since at the time the mints were considered an adult product.

The dispensers were popular and began selling all over Europe.

Not one to sit still, Haas decided to enter the burgeoning U.S. market in 1952. After two years, with U.S. sales only mediocre, he knew he had to make a change in the product. And what changes he came up with: The mints became fruit-flavored candies, and the dispensers became toys, with favorite characters on top. The result was extraordinary. PEZ took off, and Haas's American venture became a huge success.

His success became even greater when he agreed with his marketing strategists to start licensing characters for the dispensers. Popeye, beloved and famous when his PEZ dispenser appeared in 1958, was the first licensed cartoon character to be manufactured. Many more have followed, including favorite Disney and Warner Bros. characters.

As PEZ sales grew, it became clear that the company needed to manufacture its products in the United States, rather than have them imported from Europe. By the

1970s, PEZ began to be manufactured in a plant in Orange, Connecticut. Today, all dispensers sold by the company in the U.S. are manufactured in Orange, while a plant operating in Traun, Austria, creates PEZ for the rest of the world. The companies are two separate entities, but they cooperate and sometimes share production costs. Because of these two manufacturing centers, some dispensers are available for sale only in Europe, and can get in the hands of American collectors only through trading, either on the Internet or through other means. This, of course, makes them more valuable.

In the late 1980s a strange phenomenon started as a few people began getting really, really serious about collecting PEZ. The first PEZ guidebook was published in the early 1990s, and the first PEZ convention was held in 1991 in Ohio. The craze had mushroomed. Today, there are many collectors who can talk endlessly about the little

**A**t one time, you could buy a PEZ from its own vending machine. The special box the dispenser came in, shown above, included information on sending in wrappers for premiums—now highly prized.

At left is a unique PEZ clicker stamped US ZONE GERMANY. When you click it the PEZ representative offers a candy to the child. The pilot below is sporting the new look for the PEZ Pals. Reintroduced in 1996, they were available with and without coordinating body parts. Only the blond boy had the pilot's hat.

five-inch dispenser: about whether a robot or Santa Claus was the first full-bodied PEZ; about how they tracked down a 1970 pony or an early Pluto. There is a whole world of PEZ collectors sharing tips during late night phone calls, going to auctions, and visiting dealers' homes. These fans are constantly looking for the one PEZ that others have never seen; they are always waiting to be surprised by a new discovery. They decorate their basements with PEZ or have shelves of them in their bedrooms. PEZ collections have even been fought over in divorce cases. Because of this mania, the Orange plant now operates 24/7, hoping, but no doubt failing, to satisfy the insatiable needs and desires of PEZ collectors.

Today PEZ is sold in over 40 countries. And the great thing is that everyone can afford to have one. It's the toy that can put a smile on the face of a five-year-old for a dollar or an avid collector for $5,000. Everybody loves PEZ. Want one?

# Regulars

**P**EZ mints were sold in Europe in pocket tins until 1948, when the company's founder, Edward Haas, designed the convenient, hygienic dispensers we know so well. "Regulars" are the original dispensers that held the famous little mint. They came to America in the early 1950s and were sold at first as an adult item, as they had been in Europe. Many companies found the dispensers a great advertising vehicle, and had their names inscribed on the side of the stem. Executives would hand them out like calling cards. Distributors for the PEZ company would do the same, dropping the little dispenser on a desk as they left a business appointment. The early dispensers were produced in a variety of colors. None had feet, and the stems were either molded, screened, or die cut. Some had transparent stems. On the right is an early metal advertising sign. PEZ, anyone?

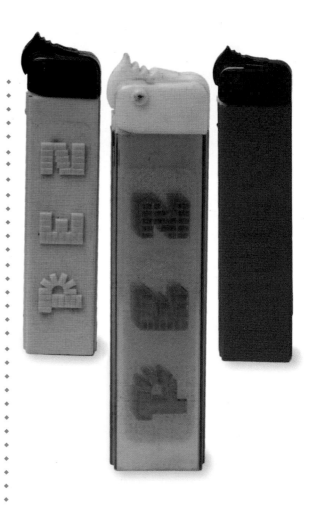

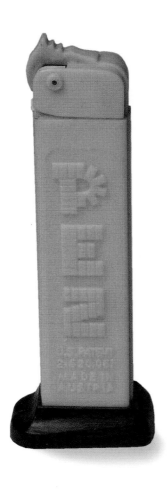
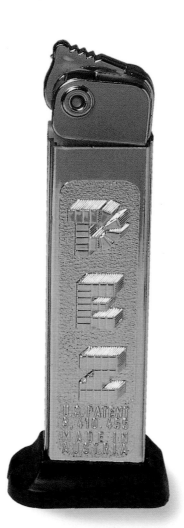

On the opposite page is a trio of early Regulars. The one in the middle has a golden hue and is called Golden Glow. Many of these early PEZ are now highly collectible, their value varying depending on the inscription. They may look a bit boring to you, but collectors have been known to dive into garbage bins to search for a really old one.

The witch at right was silk-screened. Produced in 1956, this is one of the very first dispensers distributed in the U.S. and is highly collectible.

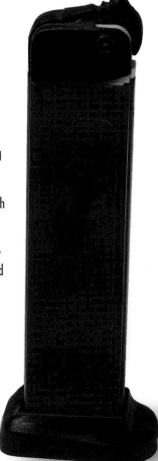

Just add a moustache and the right hat and a PEZ Pal fireman is born. Exchange these accessories for any shown on the right and enjoy your new Pal.

# PEZ Pals

PEZ Pals are fun and popular collectibles because, in the most basic sense, they are interactive. They all have the same head, with holes positioned so that moustaches, hats, and other accessories can easily be added.

PEZ Pals were born in the 1960s, when PEZ introduced Pezi Boy, a detective who travels around the world in ever-changing disguises. He is looking for his lost girlfriend, and in the process he gets involved in one mystery after another. Pezi Boy's adventures were chronicled in comic books that were included with the dispensers. Each new comic was accompanied by a Pezi Boy with a detachable disguise. Pezi Boy was a hit, and the PEZ company soon created the PEZ Pals line of dispensers.

Among the Pals were knights, maharajahs, ringmasters, a doctor, a nurse, an engineer, a fireman, a policeman, a sheik, a sailor, a sheriff, a Mexican, and a pirate. Among the most valuable is an admiral, who was made as a test but never produced en masse. The admiral is worth between $6,000 and $10,000 today.

PEZ Pals were so successful that the company named its baseball team the PEZ Pals.

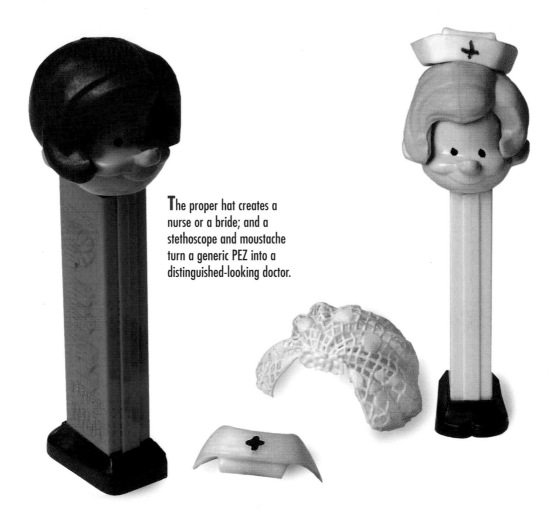

The proper hat creates a nurse or a bride; and a stethoscope and moustache turn a generic PEZ into a distinguished-looking doctor.

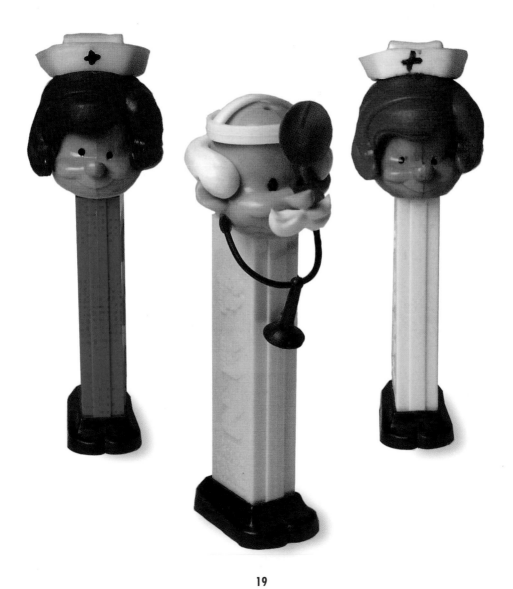

## Wedding Favors

**T**he bride and groom are very popular PEZ Pals, and one couple, Claudia and Robert, is particularly famous. This charming PEZ duo was originally created for a relative of a PEZ company employee, and only about 300 were brought to the United States as party favors for the wedding. They came in a package with an insert saying, "Claudia and Robert", and the wedding date. These are coveted collectibles today. Another happy couple is pictured at right.

*Claudia and Robert*
*October 6, 1978*

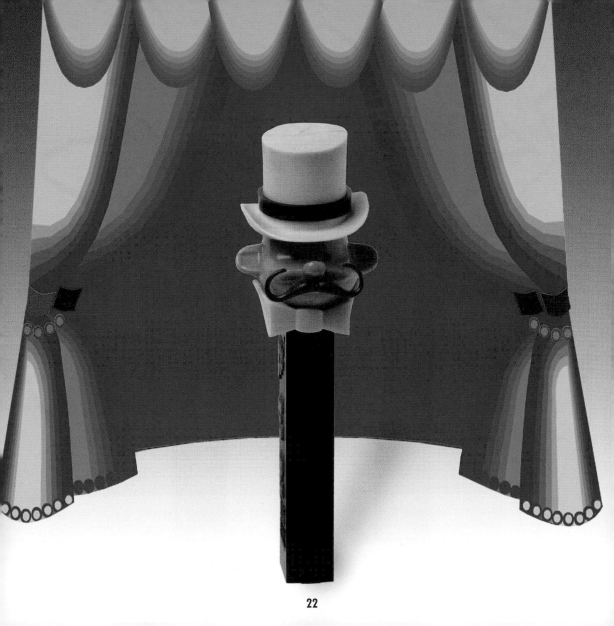

At far left is the ringmaster of the circus. On this page are two jaunty knights. The knights came in three colors: black, white, and red. The white knight is the rarest. You can tell if the knights are in their original form if the color of the plume matches the stem.

23

**B**elow left is the Alpine Man, made for the Munich Olympics and available only in Europe at the time. In the middle is the policeman, and at right is the train engineer.

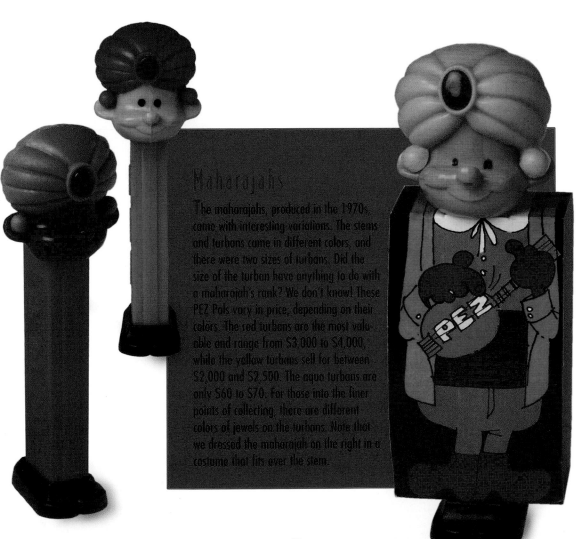

## Maharajahs

The maharajahs, produced in the 1970s, came with interesting variations. The stems and turbans came in different colors, and there were two sizes of turbans. Did the size of the turban have anything to do with a maharajah's rank? We don't know! These PEZ Pals vary in price, depending on their colors. The red turbans are the most valuable and range from $3,000 to $4,000, while the yellow turbans sell for between $2,000 and $2,500. The aqua turbans are only $60 to $70. For those into the finer points of collecting, there are different colors of jewels on the turbans. Note that we dressed the maharajah on the right in a costume that fits over the stem.

26

These PEZ Pals prove without a doubt that a little accessorizing makes a big difference. Here we have a sheik, a sheriff, a pirate, and a Mexican. The sheiks vary from $60 to $200, the sheriff from $90 to $170, and the pirate from $60 to $300. The Mexican's earrings look like coins.

27

# Die Cuts

**D**ie cuts appeared in the 1960s. The designs were cut into the stem, always revealing a different color on the sleeve underneath. This die-cut series consists of Bozo, Donald Duck, Casper, Mickey Mouse (all shown here), and Easter Rabbit. Die cuts were a short-lived experiment in making existing PEZ figures look a bit more interesting. Several were tested and did not make it into production, including a Comet with a shooting star—making that one, of course, far more valuable than the others.

# Sports

The world of sports is well represented in PEZ. A number of baseball, basketball, soccer, and football teams, both college and pro, have their own customized PEZ dispensers—and even hockey teams are represented. For that sport, it's the hockey puck that tops the stem—pretty clever!

Some of the teams with their own dispensers are the Chicago Cubs, the Orlando Magic, the Washington Wizards, the Philadelphia Kixx, the Minnesota Twins, the New Jersey Nets, and the Arizona Diamondbacks, as well as numerous minor league and college teams. The teams usually give the customized dispensers to fans in limited quantities. As collectibles, recently minted dispensers for teams are in the $30 range. The bear to the right is the Minnesota Twins mascot and dates from 2001. Next to it are two generic PEZ sports dispensers.

The football player, left, was produced in the 1960s. It can vary from $150 to $500, depending on which of the six color variations it features. The stripe on the helmet also figures into the value of the dispenser. The stripes were produced in both plastic and in tape, and for collectors the plastic, which snaps on and off, is more desirable—and more difficult to find.

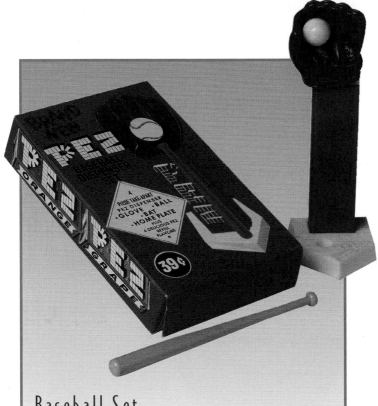

## Baseball Set

**T**he baseball set is very collectible today and a complete set is hard to come by. It was produced in the mid-1960s and came in a box. The easiest part to find is the dispenser/mitt, but since the whole set (bat, ball, and home plate) all came apart in order to make it easy to play with, many of the separate pieces have been lost.

PEZ sponsored by Du Pont Motorsports, opposite page, and the Seattle Supersonics and Philadelphia Kixx, below and right.

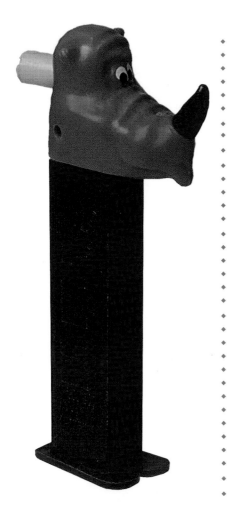

# Merry Music Makers

**M**erry Music Makers were first produced in the early 1980s and were retired in 1997. Each dispenser contained a whistle attached to the back of the head of the character. There were originally 19 different MMMs, as collectors refer to them. The Parrot, the Owl, and the Rooster all came in several colors. The Panda had painted or removable eyes and removable ears. Most of the MMMs had either no feet or had versions that were both footed and non-footed. The rarest MMM is the Owl, of which only a few are known to exist. The Owl's value ranges from $1,800 to $2,200.

**A** trio of MMMs: Left, a rhino whistle. To the right are the parrot whistle and the monkey whistle.

On this page is an MMM clown and a coach's whistle. On the right are three more MMMs: the Lamb, the Koala, and the Tiger.

# PEZ Guns

**E**ven great companies make mistakes. One of PEZ's misfires was its entry into the toy gun market with its gun dispensers. Parents were concerned about safety issues if children shot the candies into their mouths. The guns were finally discontinued and then given away as premiums. To the left is an assortment of 1950s Space Guns, in their original counter display card. To the right is a 1980s Space Gun.

# Bratz

**A**h, the Bratz! This collection is described as PEZ's "only girls with a passion for fashion." The Bratz originally consisted of only three characters, shown here, left to right: Cloe, Yasmine, and Jade. Of the three, Yasmine is the hardest to find. Sasha, far right, came later and is the rarest of all.

# Princesses

**T**he favorites of little girls everywhere, Disney's three popular princesses are also PEZ princesses. Shown here are Cinderella, Jasmine from *Aladdin,* and Belle from *Beauty and the Beast*. They first appeared in September 2005.

# Fun Facts

- The PEZ factory in Orange, Connecticut, operates 24 hours a day.
- Over 300 different PEZ dispensers have been manufactured.
- 4.2 billion pieces of PEZ candies are consumed every year.
- The company has always made its profits from the candy, not the dispensers.
- When a dispenser didn't sell well, it was either given away or sold at rock-bottom prices to organizers of country fairs or carnivals, where they could then be bought for a quarter or less.
- On occasion, when a customer sent in for one premium, he was told about another item that was available but never announced to the public. These are valuable collector's items today.
- Mickey Mouse, through the early 1990s, was always the best-selling item.
- When psychedelic eyes were produced in the 1960s, Mr. Haas insisted that the candies be flower flavored to tie in with the "flower power" theme of the times. Their taste was unpopular, and they were finally pulled off the market.

# Bugz

The happy critters that make up the Bugz series first appeared in the summer of 2000. Baby Bee, pictured horizontally above, had some subtle variations, both in color and in material. The Bugz collection includes Sweet Ladybug, shown at far left, Florence Flutterfly at near left, and Clumsy Worm at right. All Bugz have feet and are valued from $1 to $6. The Bugz were produced in Slovenia and Hungary.

45

The Bugz are nicely detailed and have very expressive faces. From left are Caterpillar, Jumpin' Jack Grasshopper, Barney Beetle, Super Bee, and Sam Snuffle the Fly.

# Eerie Spectres

**A** group of monsters and ghouls with soft heads appeared in 1979. Aptly named the Eerie Spectres, they are, from left to right, top row first on opposite page: Scarewolf, Diabolic, Vamp, Zombie, Air Spirit, and Spook. These Eerie Spectres had a very limited production and as a result are valuable today. Each figure comes in two versions, with slight color variations. One set is marked "Hong Kong," the other "Made in Hong Kong." The former is a little harder to find.

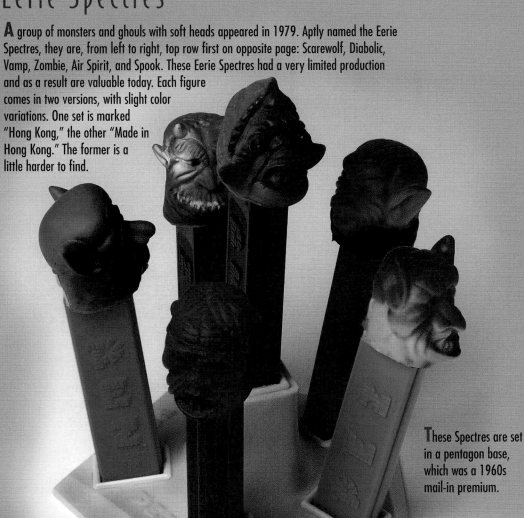

**T**hese Spectres are set in a pentagon base, which was a 1960s mail-in premium.

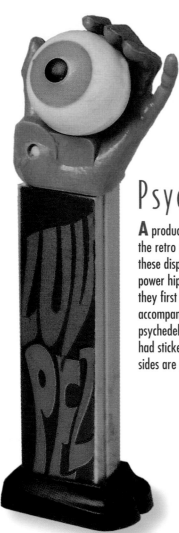

# Psychedelics

**A** product of the late 1960s (now part of the retro revival and again in production), these dispensers picked up on the flower-power hippie culture of the time. When they first came out, flower-flavored candy accompanied their Day-Glo colors and psychedelic designs. All of the dispensers had stickers; those with stickers on both sides are more valuable.

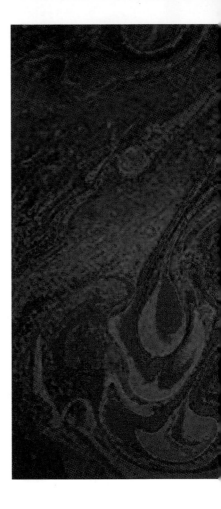

# Crazy Fruits

**T**he Crazy Fruit group came out in the mid 1970s. For some reason, the Pineapple was the least popular and was withdrawn from the market and melted down. It is therefore the rarest, and thus the most valuable. The Pear fared slightly better but is also quite rare. One Lemon was produced and is owned by a former PEZ employee; it was never mass-produced. Pictured from left are Pineapple, Orange, and Pear.

# Circus

These charming circus ponies are a favorite among collectors. The Pony is also referred to as Pony-Go-Round and comes in many color variations—heads, bridles, faces, and stems all appear in different colors. Naturally, those colors that are rarest are the most valuable, and that includes purple, pink, and green heads. There is one very special pony variation with a brown head and a rubber mane in either ivory or white. That version is worth $1,800 to $2,000.

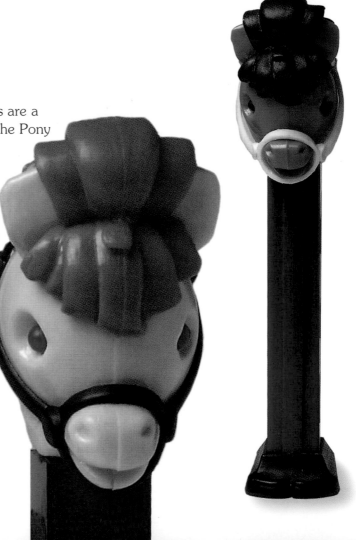

More cheery ponies are on this page. Pictured on opposite page are equally fun dispensers, the elephant and the clown. The elephant came in several color combinations and varied in another way: Some were adorned with a pointed hat, others had a flat cap, and some were bare headed. The clown whistle shown here (where there are elephants, there have to be clowns!) came with feet and with no feet.

Roar the Lion, also known as Lion with Crown, comes in many different color combinations of the stem, face, hat, mane, and eyes. It was introduced in the 1970s. Also pictured is a clown with a collar, from the 1960s. There was only one version of the giraffe produced.

# Horror

**A**t left are three Universal Studio horror characters, produced in 1965. They have wonderfully intricate detail and are very collectible. The faces are die cut. From the left, we have the handsome visages of Frankenstein, the Creature from the Black Lagoon, and Wolfman. An authentic Creature from the Black Lagoon must have the head and stem in the same color— a sickly, shimmering green color. Below is a rather engaging Mummy.

**M**ore delectable horror characters. Mr. Ugly, below, is aptly named. The Skull, in the middle, was first produced in the early 1970s and is still produced today with some variations. But no matter what they do to him, the Skull never looks healthy. The Gorilla comes in either black or dark brown.

## Make a Face

This American version of the 1970s Make a Face, based on the perennial favorite Mr. Potato Head, is extremely rare. That's because the company had to pull it off the market when serious questions about its safety were raised. The set consists of a number of small pieces, and there was fear that young children could choke on them. In addition to recalling it because of the choking hazard, the company also experienced problems with the packaging because it wasn't holding together correctly. Bottom line for collectors: This is a very rare PEZ. It is extremely hard to find a complete face with all the pieces and in its original package.

# Heroes and Villains

**T**he world has always been filled with heroes and villains, and PEZ has fine examples of both. The quintessential hero, Batman, first appeared in the PEZ world in the late 1960s. He sported a blue cape, blue mask, and blue stem. As the years went by, Batman appeared without a cape, and his ears seemed to constantly change shape. He is still produced today. Batman's colleagues appeared later.

One series was produced in the 1970s with soft heads: Batman, Batgirl, Wonder Woman, Joker, and Penguin. These are all valued at between $150 and $200 and are quite collectible.

**H**ere is Batman in his original black mask and blue stem, taken from his best angle and looking every bit the superhero. At right is Gotham's notorious villain, the Penguin. Pictured on opposite page are Joker, a soft-headed Batgirl, and a Batman with a cape.

Superheroes and villains are dramatic, fun, and irresistible. From left to right are Spiderman, Wonder Woman, the Ninja Turtle Raphael, the Green Hornet, Thor, and the Incredible Hulk.

# Changing Tastes

The first adult flavors manufactured by the PEZ company were mint, anise, eucalyptus-menthol, flower, and salmiak (a strong licorice).

In the early 1950s, to attract children to the pleasures of PEZ, cherry, lemon, lime, orange, and strawberry flavors were introduced.

PEZ began producing candies in the U.S. after 1974, and their flavors differed somewhat from the European ones, possibly because of U.S. government food regulations.

Peppermint was reintroduced in the U.S. in 1995. In 1999 a cola flavor was added everywhere but in the U.S. That became available here in 2004.

In 2002 the new sour flavors were introduced: sour blue raspberry, sour green apple, sour watermelon, and sour pineapple.

Today there are kosher PEZ.

# Valuable or Unusual

When Dustin Hoffman was told in *The Graduate* to go into plastics, his father's friend probably didn't mean PEZ; but had he started collecting back then, it would have been a very wise decision. Who could have predicted that a one-ounce, five-inch-high piece of plastic could ever be worth in the five figures? Well, some are. Naturally, the most valuable are the rarest. This year, on eBay, a clear 1950s Space Gun went for over $11,000. There is only one Admiral, and we can only imagine what he might go for at auction. The same goes for the Lemon, which was never marketed.

Coming back down to earth—and what's grittier than politics—two very valuable dispensers are the Democratic Donkey (President Kennedy was given one as a gift by the PEZ company) and the Republican Elephant. Both are from the 1960s and are estimated at $10,000 to $15,000 for the Donkey and $8,500 to $10,000 for the Elephant. These were limited editions, the ones that keep collectors up at night. Another in this same very rare category would be the Astronaut, with an inscription on the stem, from the 1982 World's Fair; that's valued at about $10,000. Only two are known to exist. One very rare and valuable PEZ, shown here at left, was made for a Lions Club meeting in Nice, France, in 1962. The Lion was specially inscribed for the meeting. Today this dispenser can fetch $2,500 or more. Later, the Lion was given a plain stem and was included in the Circus collection for commercial distribution.

# Bob the Builder

**B**ased on the very popular TV cartoon series, Bob the Builder dispensers first appeared in 2002 and are a fine example of how the PEZ company picks up on trends in the children's entertainment area.  As most kids know, from left to right are Pilchard the Cat, Wendy, Scoop (added in 2003), Bob, and Spud the Scarecrow.

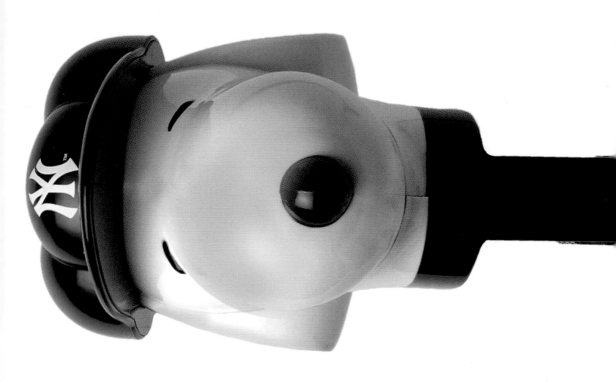

# Giant PEZ

**A**s Garfield says, "Attitude is everything." And PEZ certainly has attitude these days. The Giant PEZ, which started being produced only in the past five years, have taken off like crazy. Snoopy was the original, and he even comes in a musical version—push his hat back and he sings "Take me out to the ball game." Major League Baseball licensed him, so you can find him in your favorite team's uniform. The National Football League got in on the craze and asked PEZ to make a giant player for their teams. Eventually there were giant Muppets, Star Wars characters, Simpsons, and Santa and Easter characters. Most of them will sing to you—like Joe Cool Snoopy. But if it's just attitude you want, Giant Garfield's the one.

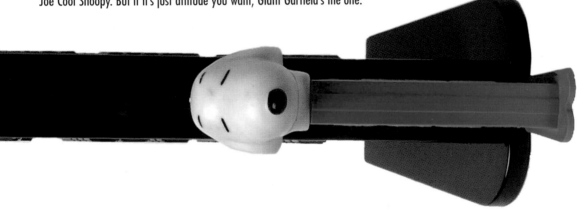

# Premiums

Premiums have been an important part of the overall marketing strategy of the PEZ company right from the beginning. In the 1950s, the company started encouraging children to save PEZ candy wrappers and send them in to get special dispensers or other products. Some of those products included glasses, masks, hats, stickers, dispenser stands, balloons, T-shirts, and pens. These premiums are highly valued by collectors today, their worth depending on whether the items are in their original package or not. Pictured at right is the premium for the movie Stand by Me, a film that mentioned PEZ.

Another favorite premium was Donkey Kong, Jr., who arrived when you mailed in an offer from a cereal box. Cheerios sent you premiums, and Cocoa Marsh sent you a free Space Gun in the 1950s. Don't like cereal? Well, if you just sent in wrappers from the candy, you could have gotten tattoos, display stands, and T-shirts.

**S**parefroh, stamped on the PEZ at right, means someone who gets pleasure from saving, in German. This PEZ appeared in the early 1970s in Europe. It was distributed on World Savings Day (October 31) and was given away by banks as a special treat for children who added to their savings accounts on that day. It is quite rare. For a while, a box of Cocoa Puffs also contained a dispenser and candy.

# Holidays

**H**olidays seem made for PEZ dispensers. Christmas, Easter, Valentine's Day—there's no limit to the designs these and other holidays inspire. Halloween is a terrific one too. In 1957 the company produced the first dispenser with a witch's head on its top. The next witch came out in 1970 with both a head and a design of a witch on one side of the stem. This second version is very difficult to find.

**O**n the opposite page, PEZ for Valentine's Day, a holiday snowman, and a cheery-looking Easter chick wearing a hat. Other Easter chicks are hatless.

## Valentines

**M**ost of the valentines are worth only $1 to $3, but some rarer ones with pink stems have gone for as much as $150.

# Easter

In a rare case of not having very cute names, these bunnies are called Bunny A and B (there is also a C). They are as hard to find as real ones are to catch. Produced in the 1950s, these are in the $200 to $500 range. They are always in this color. At far right is Baby-faced Egg.

# Halloween

The Skull first appeared in 1972 and now comes in many variations. Pumpkins were first produced in 1981 and several versions eventually reached the market. In 2002 a glow-in-the-dark series appeared; these dispensers became instant best-sellers. Pictured from left to right are the Skull, Happy Ghost, Glow in the Dark Skull, and two versions of the Pumpkin.

There are several versions of witches. The one on the right is a Glow in the Dark Witch.

## Christmas

**A** trio of favorites, PEZ-style: Winter Bear, Angel, and Reindeer.

84

## Santas

Santas have been in production since the 1950s and are among the best selling of all PEZ products. Initially Santa was full bodied, and may have been the very first PEZ produced.

Since those early days, Santa has been slimmed down to the usual stem size, but he comes with a jolly variety of heads, beards, and hats. Not surprisingly, Santa's stem is almost always red.

# Star Wars

PEZ began its Star Wars collection in 1997 with the introduction of C-3PO, Darth Vader, Storm Trooper, Yoda, and Chewbacca. They were followed in 1999 by Princess Leia, Luke Skywalker, Boba Fett, and Ewok. Then in 2002, R2-D2, Jango Fett, and a Clone Trooper were released. The most recent Star Wars characters appeared in 2005: Emperor Palpatine, General Grievous, another Chewbacca, and Death Star. All are valued under $10 and most can be purchased in set packages. A set of three crystal limited editions has been introduced, each with its own stand. Pictured from left (for the uninitiated) are Chewbacca, Emperor Palpatine, C-3PO, General Grievous, Death Star, Darth Vader, Princess Leia, and Yoda.

# The Simpsons

**T**he wacky Simpson clan became PEZ dispensers in March 2000. The whole family—Marge, Bart, Maggie, Lisa, and Homer are here, in all their bug-eyed glory.

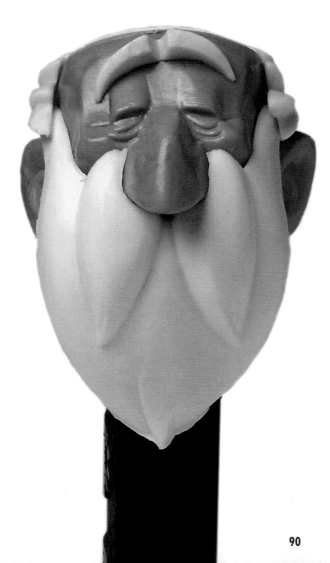

# Asterix and Friends

**A**sterix is a popular European comic book, one that adults can be seen reading without embarrassment. The story takes place in Gaul in 50 B.C. when one small village holds out against the invading Roman legionnaires and . . . well, let's just say that the Asterix characters are fun collectibles! Shown here from left to right are Muselix, Obelix, the Roman Soldier and Asterix. The original Muselix, made in the 1970s, is very valuable, in the $2,500 to $3,000 range, with the original Obelix, also produced in the 1970s, in the $1,500 to $2,000 range. The remakes, created in the 1990s, have feet and painted-on eyes and are only in the $3 to $5 range. These were not sold in the United States and are available mainly through dealers.

# Taken Off the Market

**M**ary Poppins, while beloved by book and movie fans, was not a popular character for PEZ. Produced in the early 1970s, the lively nanny looked decidedly unlively, in both her painted-cheeks and unpainted-cheeks versions. Nothing seemed to pep her up. Rumor has it that children didn't like her face, nor did Disney (and we can only imagine what Julie Andrews thought), so PEZ stopped production. Some say the company melted down the unsold dispensers. But whatever her fate, Mary Poppins dispensers are extremely rare—and the ones with painted cheeks are twice as valuable.

# Tips on Collecting

■ Read about the history of the dispensers to know when they were produced, how many were made, and what variations they came in. These are what determine price. Old PEZ dispensers did not have feet, but look carefully to make sure they haven't been filed off. Another general, but not infallible, way to determine when the dispenser was produced is to check the patent number printed on the side of each dispenser. The first two numbers tell you when it was produced: 2.6 is 1952–1968, 3.4 is 1968–1974, 3.8 is 1974–1976; 3.9 is 1976–1990; and finally 4.9 is 1990 to today. However, this is not true in every single case, since sometimes dispensers were reused or switched.

■ Check out prices on Web sites and in newsletters. A list of helpful books is included in the back of this book.

■ Go to flea markets, garage sales, thrift stores, and PEZ conventions.

■ Get to know dealers and let them know what you are looking for.

■ Older dispensers are usually more valuable, but a minimal investment in new ones, especially those that are limited, could pay off for your grandchildren. Have fun.

# Dinosaurs

**D**inosaur dispensers were first released in Europe in the 1990s, and later in the decade they came to the U.S., where they were given the family name of Pez-A-Saurs. From left are He-Saur, Fly-Saur, L-Saur, and She-Saur. The Europeans have different names for these dispensers: Chaos, Brutus, Titus, and Venezia. There are also crystal versions of these rather adorable creatures.

# Kooky Zoo

**T**he original Kooky Zoo characters came out in the 1970s in a number of color combinations. They were re-released in the late 1990s, with feet. They also were produced in crystal. Shown here are Panther, Cockatoo, Crocodile, and three cute cows. The two on either side are known as Cow A, the one in the middle Cow B.

# Uniques

**T**hese PEZ are very unusual because the whole body of the animal sits on top of the stem. The Hippo, near left, was introduced in the 1970s and is extremely difficult to find since it was distributed only in Europe and has never been released in the U.S. It fetches $1,000 and up. The Octopus, while just as unusually shaped as the Hippo, was more widely produced and thus is not nearly as valuable. It sells in the $70 to $125 range, depending on color.

The Olympic Snowman is another unusual character, since it has extended arms. It was created for the 1976 Olympics and is hard to find. It sells in the $500 range.

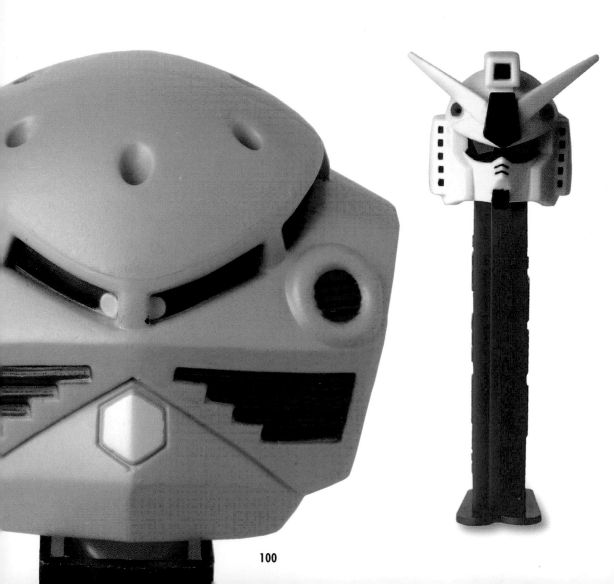

100

# Gundam

**T**hese PEZ are all part of the Gundam PEZ set, and were released only in Asia. From left are Z-Gosk, Gundam, Char's Zaku, and Zaku II.

# Licensed Characters

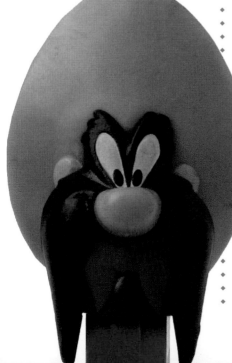

**P**EZ began producing licensed characters in the late 1950s, starting with cartoon favorite Popeye. Selecting from the most popular comics, movies, and books of the day, PEZ has created a large number of these familiar characters. Several have appeared on previous pages (Casper, Bozo, Donald Duck, and Mickey Mouse).

Shown here are some all-time favorites. Yosemite Sam appeared in the 1990s. Bert is here representing Sesame Street characters. There are also Big Bird, Elmo, Cookie Monster, Zoe, and, of course, Ernie dispensers. Sylvester was introduced in the late 1970s and comes in several versions, including a cool-looking cat in sunglasses. Of course, there's a Tweety Bird dispenser too. Pluto appeared in the 1960s. His many variations include one with movable ears.

102

**M**ore of our favorites. Olive Oyl, Popeye, and Brutus were produced from the late 1950s through the 1970s. Today they range in value from $100 to $325. Popeye had a number of different hats and several different face molds, both with and without a pipe. There was only one version each of Olive Oyl and Brutus.

**C**harles Schulz's character Charlie Brown was first produced in the 1990s. There are four versions. Shown here are Charlie Brown with a smile (in a New York Yankees cap), and Charlie Brown with his tongue showing. The other two are Charlie with his eyes closed, and Charlie with a frown (after missing the football for the umpteenth time, no doubt).

The Snow White dispenser appeared in the late 1960s. Her collar came in various colors, including turquoise, white, yellow, and green. The color of her hair bow always matched the collar color. Dopey was the only dwarf produced; he appeared with a die-cut face and in just one color.

# Dispenser Sets

**S**ome people like to collect filled counter display boxes, such as the one shown here. These vintage displays, in mint condition with wrapped dispensers, are very rare and valuable. The dispensers alone are worth from $175 to $350. One popular dispenser set was this Snow White set, with Dopey and Snow White in their wrapped packages.

**O**ther popular licensed characters include Disney's Captain Hook, Peter Pan, and Tinkerbell, all shown here. They were produced in the late 1960s.

There was a Disney set with soft heads, produced in the 1970s, that never made it to mass production. Included in this group were Mickey Mouse, Captain Hook, Donald Duck, Dumbo, Goofy, and Pluto. It's not clear why they never got produced, but only a few samples were made, making them very valuable—between $1,800 and $6,000, depending on the character. These send chills up collectors' spines.

# Garfield

**T**he well-loved and long-lived comic strip *Garfield* has its own line of dispensers featuring the smart-alecky cat. The first characters appeared in the early 1990s and included three different Garfields—one plain, one with teeth, and one with a visor—as well as his girlfriend Arlene and two versions of his nephew Nermal. The second series came later in the decade and featured a plain Garfield, Garfield falling asleep, Garfield dressed as a chef, Arlene looking considerably less vampy than her original incarnation, and Odie, pretty much being Odie. While extremely cute, the Garfield collection is not of great value to collectors.

From left are plain Garfield, Sleepy Garfield, Aviator Garfield, and Chef Garfield, all from the second series.

111

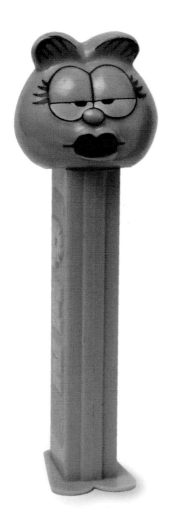

Garfield's nemesis Odie, far left, is from the second series of Garfield characters, while the first series is represented on this page with a vampy Arlene and one of the two Nermals produced in the early 1990s.

Childhood favorite Winnie-the-Pooh is a well-loved PEZ character. First made in the 1970s and released in Europe, the character was introduced into the U.S. market in 2001. Bullwinkle first appeared in the 1960s, with both a yellow stem and the now rare brown stem. To the right are Minnie Mouse, Donald Duck, and Daisy Duck.

The classic Sanrio Hello Kitty PEZ has a red stem and a white head. She appeared in Europe in 2003 and didn't migrate to the U.S. until the following year. Today Kitty is made with a crystal head.

The movie *Madagascar* has spawned a menagerie of animals, including Gloria the Hippo, Marty the Zebra, and Alex the Lion. They have terrific faces and great detail. The Giraffe and the Penguin won't come out until 2007. All are licensed from Dreamworks.

# Full-bodied Robots

**T**he very first PEZ dispenser produced was full bodied. There is a debate as to whether it was a Santa figure or a robot. Whichever it was, the early full-bodied robots, created in the 1950s, are very difficult to locate. Even though the full-bodied dispensers were popular, the decision was made early on to switch to a straight rectangular body. The robot, also known as Spacetrooper, was produced in four colors. The red, blue, and yellow robots are valued between $300 and $550, but the Gold Robot is extremely rare and is valued at over $2,000.

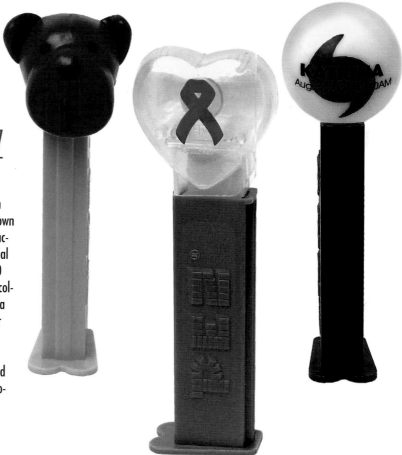

# Charity PEZ

**P**EZ frequently creates dispensers for charities to use in their fund-raising efforts. Shown here is Barky Brown, manufactured for the Australian Animal Welfare League. Only 10,000 were produced, with various colored stems. Next to Barky is a PEZ created for Breast Cancer Awareness, with all proceeds going to the Susan G. Komen Breast Cancer Foundation. And next to that is a dispenser produced to help the victims of Hurricane Katrina.

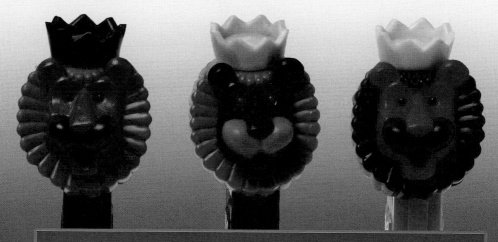

# PEZ Variations

■ Right from the beginning, the PEZ company did variations of their dispensers. For example, the early Zorro PEZ was produced with the logo engraved on the side of the stem, and another was done without the logo. The four die cuts—Casper, Mickey Mouse, Donald Duck, and Bozo—were also produced without the die-cut stem. Obviously, the harder a variation is to find, the more valuable it is.

■ Another major variation is in the head. The same mold was often produced, but it was made with different face colors, or sometimes with varied removable parts. The ponies and maharajahs, for example, were produced with color variations in the stem and the head, and even some of the features on the head differed. Some early dispensers, including the PEZ Pals, were issued with two different molded heads. Batman has been produced with at least six different heads and a number of color variations.

■ Another major variation concerns the feet: Some dispensers were made both with and without them.

■ Each difference can affect the price.

## Trucks

**F**our series of trucks came out starting in the late 1970s, and more were produced in the 1980s and early 1990s. Some, like the Walgreens truck, were promotional. They come in a seemingly endless array of color combinations. Some are worth only $1; others fetch in the $450 range.

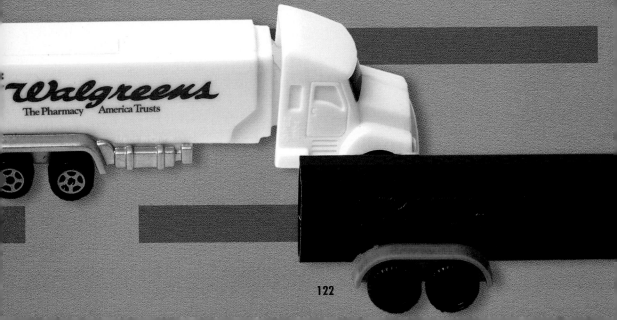

Walgreens
The Pharmacy America Trusts

# Heroes

**P**EZ has released special dispensers in response to a number of natural disasters and tragedies. This group of Emergency Heroes was released in the U.S. to honor all of those men and women who responded to the terrible events of September 11. Represented are air force pilots, nurses, firemen, construction workers, policemen and policewomen, Army Rangers, Navy Seals, and K-9 German shepherds. It was a wonderful salute by PEZ to all those who risked their lives and exhibited extraordinary courage.

**T**o the left is the Army Ranger, and to the right are K-9 German shepherd, the Policewoman, and the Fireman.

Because of their significance, Emergency Heroes are popular collectibles. Shown here are, from left, Air Force Pilot, Nurse, Fireman, Construction Worker, and Navy Seal Scuba Diver.

# Bicentennial

**T**he PEZ company helped celebrate America's Bicentennial in 1976 by producing a very American cast of characters. Both Uncle Sam and Betsy Ross are looking very serious indeed. The equally solemn-looking Indian Brave and Indian Maiden were joined by an Indian Chief. The Chief's headdress came in a large variety of colors. The legend goes that the Make a Faces that never sold were melted down and recycled for the headdresses, which explains the variety of marbleized colors. Even so, these figures were not very successful and were later sold as part of assortment packs.

# SOURZ

**P**EZ Sourz have candies with a really tangy taste. And while the dispensers may look as though you would never want to eat their candy, they are very popular and several have sold out.

From left are Sour Raspberry (in package), Sour Green Apple, Sour Pineapple, and Sour Watermelon. Enjoy!

# Crystal Heads

The PEZ company began producing crystals in the 1990s. The beautiful, clear-headed dispensers are often crystal versions of already existing molds. Pictured here are the Lion, Sour Pineapple, Clear Pumpkin, Clear Elf, and Hippo.

# Minis

For the few people in the world who don't smile when they see a regular size PEZ, they surely will when gazing at a mini. Miniature PEZ are found mainly in Japan, where they are sold in vending machines and are generally released for only a short period of time. An insert accompanies the dispensers, and both are placed in a bag or box. The minis come with the same size candy as the regular dispensers, but half as much. Japanese mini PEZ are generally traded over the Internet.

The mini PEZ is about half the size of its big brother. To the left is the Pokémon character Pikachu, shown standard size and mini. On this page is Henry from *Thomas the Tank Engine* and Rody meets Frog.

These minis are, from left, Gachapin (part of Gachapin and Mukku, a set of five); Kanegon (part of the Ultra Man III mini dispenser set); and P-Chan (part of the Gachapin and Mukku set).

**S**uper Saiyan Goku and Vegeta are
characters from the Dragonball-Z
mini series.

These minis are, from left, Piccolo, Krillin, and Frieza, part of the Dragonball-Z mini dispenser set.

When it comes to adorableness, it's hard to beat these minis. The fuzzy farm animals are versatile: They dispense candies, of course, and they are handy little key chains too.

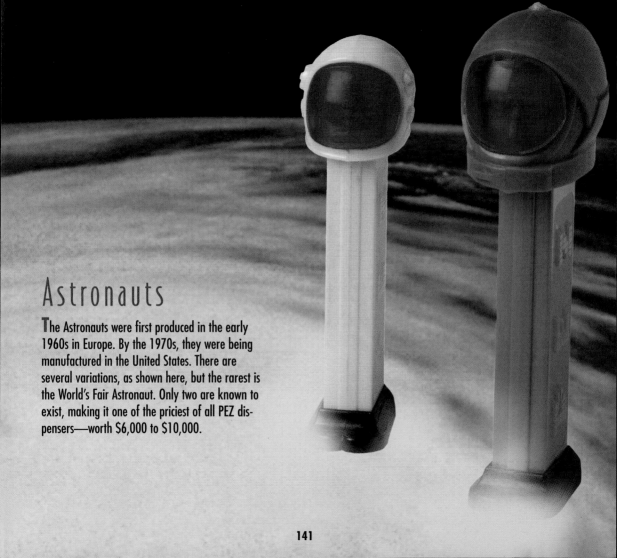

# Astronauts

**T**he Astronauts were first produced in the early 1960s in Europe. By the 1970s, they were being manufactured in the United States. There are several variations, as shown here, but the rarest is the World's Fair Astronaut. Only two are known to exist, making it one of the priciest of all PEZ dispensers—worth $6,000 to $10,000.

# Index

# Celebrating Our Collector

We are grateful to **John LaSpina** for allowing us to photograph a small part of his vast, colorful PEZ collection, and for providing us with so much fascinating information.

John has been an avid PEZ collector for over sixteen years. He is the author of the *Original Collector's Price Guide to PEZ*, which is currently in its 17th edition. He collects everything PEZ-related and attends most of the PEZ conventions. John not only buys and collects PEZ, he sells them too. You can visit his Web site at http://home.att.net/~jjpezpal

John wishes all readers Happy PEZing!

---

**The following books and articles were instrumental in the writing of this book:**

Belyski, Richie, *PEZ Collectors' News*

Geary, Richard, *PEZ Collectibles*, Schiffer Publishing LTD., 1994

LaSpina, John J., *The Original Collector's Price Guide to PEZ*, Spring 2006

Peterson, Shawn, *Collector's Guide to PEZ*, Wisconsin, Krause Publications, 2003

Peterson, Shawn, *Warman's PEZ Field Guide*, Wisconsin, Krause Publications, 2004

Welch, David, *Collecting PEZ*, Bubba Scrubba Publications, 1996

Welch, David, *A Pictorial Guide to Plastic Candy Dispensers Featuring PEZ*, Bubba Scrubba Publications, 1991

Photograph on page 7: © Robert Levin/CORBIS

**Barbara J. Morgan**  Publisher
**Leonard Vigliarolo**  Design Director
**Robert Milazzo**  Photography
**Jane F. Neighbors**  Copy Editor
**Gina Graham**  Editorial Assistant
**James Trimarco**  Art Assistant
**Della R. Mancuso**  Production

The PEZ dispensers featured in this book
are from the fine collections of
John LaSpina and Nina Chertoff.